T0148357

Because You
DESERVE A BOOK

NYASHA LESURE

BECAUSE YOU DESERVE A BOOK

iUniverse books may be ordered through booksellers or by contacting:

iUniverse
1663 Liberty Drive
Bloomington, IN 47403
www.iuniverse.com
1-800-Authors (1-800-288-4677)

Because of the dynamic nature of the Internet, any web addresses or
links contained in this book may have changed since publication and
may no longer be valid. The views expressed in this work are solely those
of the author and do not necessarily reflect the views of the publisher,
and the publisher hereby disclaims any responsibility for them.

Any people depicted in stock imagery provided by Getty Images are
models, and such images are being used for illustrative purposes only.
Certain stock imagery © Getty Images.

ISBN: 978-1-5320-9050-9 (sc)
ISBN: 978-1-5320-9051-6 (e)

Print information available on the last page.

iUniverse rev. date: 12/04/2019

The Mind
A blank canvas filled by the memories you store

The body
A physical experience of everything that lingers on the flesh

The soul
A permanent accumulation of what has
created who you are as a being

MIND

Nyasha LeSure

reality- seven letter that will never quite make sense

november 27th, 2015

i was lying in bed trying to take a nap after pregame and you had just gotten out of the shower. you laid in bed wrapped in your towel and kissed me. you asked me to officially be your girlfriend.

i wish i had said no then.

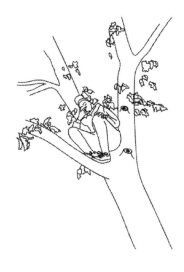

my strength comes from my struggle

and

my struggle starts and ends with

you.

i am truly sorry for how unlovable i was when all you wanted to do

was love me

slowly but surely i have learned that life isnt about who they were, its about how they made you feel. you have to hold on to those moments that made you feel like the world was perfect in that moment even if its just for a second. i thank you for all the perfect seconds you gave me.

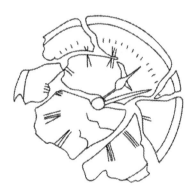

it makes me sad that

even now

     on some days

the thought of you is the only reason i smile.

you were like smoke

beautiful in your movement

but in seconds

       evaporated

into thin air

you took it as the universe saying

stop or it will continue to hurt

                     i took it as the universe yelling

                     don't stop until you stop hurting

     i guess its just difference in perspective.

i would rather be hopelessly in love than

        hopelessly alone

i would rather a lie keep me warm at night than

        the cold cold truth

i would rather the thought of you than

        the thought of losing you

i would rather leave this earth than

        live another day without you.

i cant imagine myself using love in its past tense form when it comes to you

but then again

      ive never had much of an imagination

you broke me. and not in the chunky pieces kind of way. in the way that when you shatter glass the pieces spray. the way i love you has a power that cannot be explained to a simple mind . the way i love you has had to develop over time. it has no rhythm or rhyme. it makes no sense. it keeps us in constant suspense.

it was a love that was so easy but intense.

a love that was uncontainable but forced to be condensed. car sick is an understatement when speaking openly. love is an unspoken plea. like the whistle of the wind through the leaves of a tree .fully invested in someone that is an absentee. completely and utterly alone. just wanting a future with someone to call my own.to make a house a home but the windows in that house have started to crack. demonstrating the invariable attacks on my heart. im then forced to use self-defense to clarify the reasoning behind the unchanging hurt. the ceaseless pain. the infinite chain.

the reason why i constantly settle for less in my brain.

you have caused me to go insane.

i think its just easier to love you.

its easier to care,

      admitting to myself who you really are,

   now that's hard.

understanding that you walked away and learned from me as if i was just another mistake.

    purely knowing that the person you love the most could care less about the next breath you take.

      now that's hard.

you came into my life,

lit a fire

    then watched as it burned down everything in its path

i fall asleep with a broken heart. begging God to ease the thought of you. please take away these memories that have me so defeated . give me peace of mind. a heart no longer longing for what is in the past. i drift into a deep abyss of hell but hell is not built of fiery flames. hell is the brown of your eyes. hell is the warmth of your touch. the indulgent look of your lips. hell is the sin of your kiss. my dreams go deeper into your creamy caress. the soothing sound of your seductive speech. strumming my heart with your fingers as if you were playing the most delicate harp God's hands had ever created.

i wake up in love

in love with the past

in love with you all over again

i wake up in a false love

i wake up in hell.

i will never understand how i could love something so bad for me

i finally understand the term addiction

i miss the days where you were my friend

i was your person and you were mine

    i miss those days

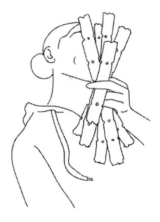

im protective of your heart

      i will always protect it with everything i have

man, i wish i felt as passionately for my own heart.

my eyes are heavy with tears of the past. im tired but i cant sleep ever since the thought of life crossed my mind. the delicate idea of growing up and growing old seems to be taking a toll. the words that come to my head when i try to define my love for you are bottomless, endless like the numbers that start with one and end with infinity but even numbers arent infinite. see im not much of a poet and my lines don't flow like water from a forever flowing faucet but loving you gave me my first exquisite experience of my heart stopping. a permanent pulsation stopped by the first time you uttered the words 'i love you', i never knew such a simple saying could mean so much but i soon understood that we defined this elementary phrase differently, for your definition of love is a list of feelings you dare not speak. so as time ticked by i found my way to your heart but the sweet taste of our potential vanished. vanished like a thief in the night. i never knew how much i loved you until i made the decision to love someone else as intensely as i love you.

so if there is one thing i have learned

learned from loving, learned from being loved by you and learned from losing you.

i would rather be alone than loving someone else.

so until you are ready.

i will lay here and think of a million little memories i cant wait to share with you

Nyasha LeSure

why cant love be black and white?

i have decided that gray is my least favorite color

how am i so forgettable when everything reminds me of you?

we are like two cars racing on the freeway just to be stopped

at the same red light

both at a different pace but end up at the same altar in all white.

to you i was a mistake

an accident

a misstep

to me you were everything

a partner

a future

Nyasha LeSure

my breathing still catches every time i hear your name

and all i think is that i hope you're doing okay.

one day at 11:11 i will have nothing else to wish for

you will be everything i wanted

and i will have nothing more to ask for.

BODY

you have this thing you do

where you smile right before you say

            "youre not funny"

that's my favorite smile.

may 25th, 2018

i told myself that if we were still dating by november 27th, 2018,
i was going to propose

i just want my head on your chest

                struggling to match your breathing

listening to your heart start to race

that sound

      is the sound of you falling in love with me again.

i cannot comprehend the idea of letting my heart heal from
loving you

the idea seems so foreign when the thing that i need to heal
from

        is the one thing that holds me together

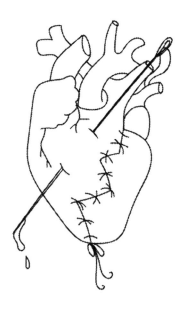

as soon as the flakes started to fall from the sky, i knew it was time to bundle up. for as soon as the ground was white id hear "lets go on an adventure." and how could i say no to a smile as white as the fresh winters snow?

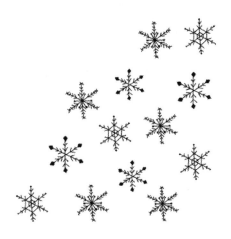

Nyasha LeSure

once i learned to sleep on my own

        i noticed your presence was no longer in my shirt

      i could finally sleep without your arm around me in bed

     for once

       i could finally move freely

you have completely and utterly taken charge of my heart

you are in full control

regardless of the struggles ive endured

trying to regain dominance of this disloyal organ of mine.

Nyasha LeSure

you offer me your chapstick and i take it

without hesitation

    i know thats the closest ill ever get to your lips again

i thought you leaving would make it easier.

but i guess its true what they say

        distance makes the heart grow fonder.

Nyasha LeSure

i want to love her how i loved you,

problem is, i don't know if im capable of putting myself back in the line of fire again

love is a shootout,

        we either both surrender

                or one dies.

you were the air that filled my lungs

and

now

i feel as though the wind has been knocked out of me

you are a constant reminder of the way i deserve to be loved

you showed me every way i do not deserve to be loved.

an addict by definition is 'an enthusiastic devotee of a specific thing.' sort of like a kite at the end of someone elses string. constantly trying to chase that first high. the first moment i felt as though i could fly. like i would never die. constantly dismissing reason as though it does not apply. i start to understand that i am craving a vibration.

a pulsation.

a simple sensation.

that is nothing more than an unhealthy fixation.

so i find the strength to move forward from this addiction that has carried such a negative connotation. because when i look in the mirror my hearts reflection has been lost in translation. i rack my brain for the road less traveled. trying to make sense of the day it all unraveled. but every memory is filed under that smile and those eyes. not realizing that those beautiful features were a disguise. masking all the cries.

the lies.

i relay this message of an addict in a way that seems so cruel. because without you right now. i have no fuel. you are my drug and the memories are my plug and my mind is a box that i am trapped in and its getting pretty snug. my thoughts, my memories have become my worlds maps. in reality my world is about to collapse but i chose to remember things how i want which causes traps. it causes my judgement to lapse.

then i relapse.

i am enthusiastically devoted to the pain.

the days of endless rain. until ive finally gone completely insane. i am in recovery. which is a forever thing. as permanent as clipping a birds wing or getting on one knee with a ring. so i will forever be stuck in my own mind as

your personal plaything.

november 27th, 2018

(well, im single)

i hurt when you hurt so even though we are apart

i hope your heart is safe

Nyasha LeSure

you came in like

a light breeze

                    you left like a

thunderstorm

when you said

                       never

i though it broke me

but it finally gave me the strength to realize

i deserve

much

        much

better.

SOUL

finally trying to grasp a future without you.

that was the problem with our love

we confused dependency with unconditional.

we completed each other instead of complimenting one another

you stayed on the phone with me until i promised to stay on
this earth.

i owe you every breath after.

you made me feel something ive never felt before

twice

1. completely whole

2. forever broken

i was broken,

      you were broken

you helped me put myself back together

adding pieces of you where spaces were empty

      then you walked away

leaving me to figure out what pieces of you

      i can live without

you deserved more than what i could give then

but you deserve everything i can give to you now

im sorry for that.

i loved you but found out i was in it alone. i was choosing to binge on every memory of you. until you said the word never. i then found the strength to remove you from my life. now all i dream about is your touch. and out of habit i fall in love with you all over again.

i was enough

      i am enough

i will always be enough

I am just too much for you.

and thats okay.

I will continue to repeat this to myself until

i believe its true.

i will continue to search the bottom of each bottle until i find the answer i am looking for.

begging you to not leave because i knew what your plans were

was the lowest point of my life

it felt like i was losing my only connection to this world

thank you for staying

even if it meant you leaving me.

its weird how we all have our drug of choice

mine is you.

but yours was never me.

that's the thing about addiction, it's a one-sided battle

is it too crazy of a concept to think that loving you forever is the most stable thought in head?

that the thought of losing you takes me back to the bottom of a bottle and the drivers seat of my car?

becasue i truly love you

more than i love me

or i wouldnt continue to do this to myself.

who would have thought putting myself first

would be my greatest struggle?

your laugh at 2am

the one that comes straight from the bottom of your stomach

the one that radiates the very definition of happiness

yeah, thats my favorite laugh

i would give anything to hear it just one

last

time.

just to completely heal my heart.

never give up

continuing to chase that feeling because

you deserve it

the moment i decided to take my own life

you were my last thought

and in the moment, i realized

youre not worth it.

a moment of clarity

you saved me from a bottle of pills

just to put me in a bottle for your amusement

i hope youre enjoying the show

i love our crazy...

i miss our crazy...

never- five letters that are so definitive

i wish i knew

the last time was the

last time.

if i had a gun to my head—you're still the person id call

if that means anything to you

because you don't think i deserve a sorry

i guess its time for me to accept the apology

i

will

never get...